THOUGHTS TO THINK BY!

Blessings in your life change!
Shirley Burdick
"Empathy"
1-29-2019

BY FRANK V. SCHIMANSKI

ILLUSTRATIONS AND PICTURES:
BY SHIRLEY BURDICK

Copyright © 2002 by Frank V. Schimanski

ISBN 978-0-7414-1022-1

Published by:

1094 *New DeHaven Street, Suite 100*
West Conshohocken, PA 19428-2713
Info@buybooksontheweb.com
www.buybooksontheweb.com
Toll-free (877) BUY BOOK
Local Phone (610) 941-9999
Fax (610) 941-9959

Printed in the United States of America

Published December, 2012

TABLE OF CONTENTS

ABOUT THE AUTHOR

I was born on Christmas Day in 1932 to God-fearing parents. Those Christmas values have stayed with me all my life.

My best Christmas present was my brother born nine years later, also on Christmas Day!

I've tried in this book to share my thoughts and to challenge yours, to share my answers and to challenge yours, and to challenge all of us to always seek out the truth and find God's -peace!

~~~~~~~~~~~~~~~~~~

I wrote this book for me myself. I needed to write down my feelings and thoughts on paper and to see and read them back.

It has been a blessing to explore and challenge my mind! It has strengthened my faith and helped me find God's peace, I wish to share that with you!

~~~~~~~~~~~~~~~~~~~~~~~~~~~

If there are such a things as words of wisdom or wisdom in words, then I challenge you to read and to share yours! My words are only the beginning of thought; your answer is the wisdom, and only wisdom shared has any real value!

1

I dedicate this book to those like me, who feel the need, at times, for an encouraging word.

This author makes no claim to know the answers. I do know the one who does. My words, here in put together, are meant to serve to brighten your day and give you hope and peace!

Sincerely,
Frank V. Schimanski

To those who's kind hearts and talents have made this book possible:

Shirley Burdick, for illustrations and word processing beyond compare!

Elaine Flathers, the proofreader with a heart!

Jim Waddell, the computer programmer expert and friend!

To you all I give my humble thanks and praise!

2

AS THE SUN RISES!

A BRIGHT NEW DAY

I opened my eyes to a bright new day,
fresh snow had fallen on the hay!
The fields were covered with the
blanket of white that had fallen so quietly
thru the night!
A bright, clean display so bold, making
it all a wonder to be to behold.
So challenge the day and live it all.
Never worry or fuss or think of a fall!

THE DAWN BREAKS

As the dawn breaks, and pieces of sun light up the world, people put together their day. New light is shed on the young and the old, causing excitement for those who are bold!

Stand your square, and you'll get there; let the Lord be your guide.

Your rewards will be for all to see, and you'll live your life with pride.

****
OPEN DOOR OF A NEW DAY

I've opened the door of a new day, the misty rays of light flow gently past the frame of that door into my house. The day and the light have taken over. The day has officially begun!

I look out into the beginning light to see that I am not alone. Down the street a neighbor gets into his car; another drives by. A couple sharing a morning walk, talking and walking, as if they were the only two people in the world!

One of the neighbor dogs begins his good morning bark. Soon his many friends bark their greetings! A squirrel hops across the snow hitting his tree safely and then rises above it all!

Early birds are doing their thing; my eyes and ears are filled with sounds and motion!

The cold air brings me out of my temporary moment, and I close the door!

Inside, the warmth of the house makes me count my blessings over again: the breakfast I fix, the comfort of my chair, the warm clothes when I go out, and on and on...........

Thank you, Lord, for this new day!

****

✝ MORNING CAME ✝

*Morning came again! Where am I? I have
not been here before! God has blessed me with another
day!*

*God has blessed me with many new days.
God has been with me each of those days and will be with
me today!*

*As I open my eyes and see the brightness of the day,
as I breath the breathe of life that God gives me, as I
touch the comfort of my bed, and smell the sweetness of the
air, I thank my Lord for all His blessings!
I live; I have life; and I may serve my Lord. Thanks
be to God!
God will listen to my prayers. God will answer my
prayers. God will guide me through my day!
Whatever my need, God is all I need! Amen*

LIFE

Life begins; life rises; life sets!

In the beginning of our lives we reflect the glow of our parents' pride; we rise to shine on our own. When twilight comes, we bathe in the afterglow!

Our Lord provides the light of the sun that our lives need from beginning to sunset, light that all things living need to grow and flourish, light that we may see the path we must take in His service.

May the light of the Son of God surround you with His presence, with the warmth of His rays, so that when the sun sets on our earthly lives, the afterglow of memories will provide peace and joy, knowing that when the Son rises again, He will shine on all of us together!

THOUGHTS

The wind composed its own melody as it sounded through the window. I sat listening to its concert this early morn, before daylight had a chance to enter the room.

Along with the wind, the rain added its own beat as it hit the window. The symphony of sound played just outside my room as I sat warm and dry, comfortable and secure.

The quiet of the inside made me think of how close real differences are; a window, a wall, a thought, an action, a night and day, at the drop of a moment in time.

We need to remember how easy things can change. We need also to realize that a change from good to bad can also be from bad to good.

Each moment in time is its very own, each new moment is brand new, if each new now moment is to have real meaning and become a good memory it must be used to the best of its own ability.

Let the wind blow and the rain beat its time on the window; and as we listen to life's symphony let us remember the melody of peace and share it!

LIGHTEN UP

I woke up this morning, the sky looked gray. I
asked myself would it stay that way?

Who needs a day with shades of gray, no one should
have to face a day that way.

So I took a second look and lo and behold, there was
A break in those clouds that I did behold!

The warmth of the sun came shinning thru, it did
for me, it can for you!

For clouds are only a cover up, for a sunny day. The
Son of God is always there to brighten our way!

~~~~~~

AM – Lord I thank you for bringing me to the beginning of
this new day. Make me equal to its tasks and challenges
and surround me with thy love and thy strength as I try
to live this day for thee!

In thy name we pray,

Amen.

A.M.

Good morning Lord! Its another day, another day for you to guide me along my life's way.

I notice some changes in the way things work, but I know your always there! Your duty you do not shirk!

I feel your strength and love at early mornings light!
I know your there beside me when troubles are in sight!
The wonder of your presence fill my heart with joy.
Your promise of eternal life I know is the real McCoy.
Thank you Lord for being there for me.
Through all life's problems whatever they may be!

Amen

P.M.

Evening has come and now its time to rest
Another day is over Lord and I have done my best.
I've tried to live as you want me to.
I've tried because I do love you!
Thank you now for this past day,
And for your presence along the way!
Grant me now a good nights sleep,
As I know your love I can always keep!

Amen

A.M.

As the dark of night gives way to the bright new day;
Lift my spirits Lord, show me the way!

Open my eyes that I may see; just what you want me to do and to be.

Open my heart and mind to receive, your strength and love that I will believe.

Bless you, Lord, and thanks from my heart, to give my life this brand new start!

In thy name I pray. Amen!

P.M.

The shades of night are coming down; daylight is coming to an end.

If at this time I am alone; I know I always have you as my friend.

Take the burdens of my day, anxiety, aches and pain, turn them into quiet sleep, that a good nights rest I will gain.

Thank you, Lord for always being there, and answer to my every prayer!

Amen.

WORLD GRAY

When the world seems gray, and nothing seems to go right,
Take a deep breath, talk to God, pray that gray out of sight!
God hears your words right from the start.
He also hears those in your heart
So share with Him the color of your life, and
he will cut away that gray with His heavenly knife,
So that tinted and refreshed, the color will return
by the grace of God, a blessing we can not earn.
Live in that color and do what is right, and
keep God's rainbow always in sight!

14

SCENES OF LIFE

WINTER OF LIFE

Empty limbs reaching out in the winter of life from a trunk all
knotted and gnarled.
Age passing, now taking a rest till enough strength is gained
to put forth new leaves.
The sundown of the day, the sundown of life comes to all; yet
still beauty can be seen.
The tree with all its rugged edges still shows the strength and
dignity of its maker.
The sun setting, leaving such a warm glow, will rise again
to share its strength and light.
Wherever we are in this earthly life; however the shape of our
limbs, we know our life is like the sunset, that we will again rise
to eternal life.
So praise our Lord, and if we need to rest once in a while-fine,
we know we will bear new leaves in God's heaven!
Keep the faith!

THE BARE TREE

Bare arms filled with bony elbows reaching toward the sky.

"Where, oh, where are my leaves?" they were heard to cry.

"Why, its winter," said the Lord.. It's time for you to rest!

"For when spring comes, I want you to look your best.

"You'll need them all, and I'll give them to you.

"You will need them all for what I want you to do.

"Shade the children as they play; shade the parents on their way.

"Shade the strollers as they walk; hear their conversation as they talk.

"Shade those with gentle age, as their pace is not so fast.

"Shade them well; let them rest, as you help them toward their last.

"Young and old will need your shade as you stand with the leaves you have made.

"Cry not now as your bony elbows reach toward the sky!"

Remember well the words of God as he has told you why!

God has his reasons; they are always for our good.

So put your limbs in His – you are more than just a pile of wood!!

THE CHARACTER TREE

The beauty of winters frost, shown thru this tree and its time lost.

All twisted broken and bent, signs of a history well spent.

Yet in its gnarls and its pain, still new limbs do grow and remain, as if to say in its own special way, "I still have life for another day, for when again spring does come, to erase all of winter's glum, I'll show that new life and new hope, an example for your life to help you cope"!

The gnarls of age may get you down, but you need not face the future with a frown, shoot up new branches, sponsor new life, overcome your strife!

Winter frost will melt away and you will have a brand new day!!!

FROST FOREST

Frost gets together, its beauty to share with the
limbs of trees that are now bare.
Forming a forest of feathery trees, this work of
God has been done with ease!
Inspiration and beauty, gifts of love, gifts of
our heavenly father above!
God gives the seasons, inspires the change.
He will help us all our lives to arrange!
We need only faith, and then to ask our Lord
for help with our task!!
His wisdom and presence never rare
His love and strength to always share.
The frosty beauty of this forest bare
does remind us always, God is there!!!

BIRD UPON A HILL

There is a bird upon the hill, sitting there of its own free will!

Strutting now to and fro, waiting for its time to go.

Independent, this bird I see, not like others like to be.

Confident and full of pride, for now another eagle is by his side!

EMPTINESS

Open door, open window,

emptiness all around.

Wonderful temperature, wonderful scenes,

emptiness all around.

Comfortable chair, going no where,

emptiness all around.

Neither hungry nor thirsty, just

emptiness all around.

The stillness brings quiet sounds from

distant traffic on the road.

The stillness shouts of loneliness. That's not

a happy mode.

I think the real value in peace and quiet is

being able to share it!

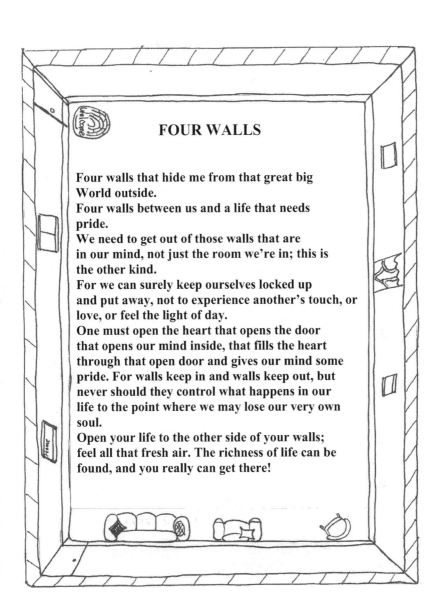

FOUR WALLS

Four walls that hide me from that great big
World outside.
Four walls between us and a life that needs
pride.
We need to get out of those walls that are
in our mind, not just the room we're in; this is
the other kind.
For we can surely keep ourselves locked up
and put away, not to experience another's touch, or
love, or feel the light of day.
One must open the heart that opens the door
that opens our mind inside, that fills the heart
through that open door and gives our mind some
pride. For walls keep in and walls keep out, but
never should they control what happens in our
life to the point where we may lose our very own
soul.
Open your life to the other side of your walls;
feel all that fresh air. The richness of life can be
found, and you really can get there!

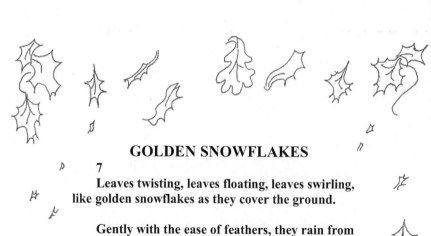

GOLDEN SNOWFLAKES

7

Leaves twisting, leaves floating, leaves swirling,
like golden snowflakes as they cover the ground.

Gently with the ease of feathers, they rain from
the trees to the ground where they just lie around.

They are for children to play in, pets to run in,
and squirrels to frolic in, while Dads see nothing but
work.

The yard is filled with the rainbow beauty of fall
colors just waiting for Dad, his work not to shirk.

Watching the fall in the fall as summer season
comes to an end,
we give thanks for the summer as if it were an
old friend.

For the grace and peace in this fall
season, we give thanks to God, for He
is the reason!

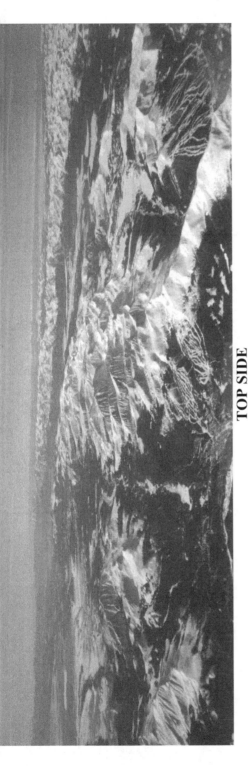

TOP SIDE

The wonders of our earth as seen from the top, peaks full of snow, of numbers non-stop!

As far as our eyes can see are the marvels of God's creation for you and for me.

Breath- taking beauty from heights that take your breath away, unrivaled by man, yet given by God each day. Given for us and in our lives to embrace and enjoy, a reminder of our Lord and his power to employ!

WHITE FEATHERY BRANCHES

*Pure-white feathery branches gently wave in reverence
to the God that gave them such beauty!*

Our summer purpose gone, our winter service shared!

*Thank you, my, Lord for your presence ever in our lives
showing us that even barren branches can be a source of
pride.*

*Lord, how often we feel like barren branches with little
purpose and value. Thank you for your reminder that
you can bring out the values we have within us, that
we can lift them up and with reverence share them with
the world around us! Praise God!*

TALL AND STRAIGHT

*Tall and straight I may not be, but God has
put me here for all to see!
Renewing my life and letting me grow, giving
me the chance my seed to sow!*

OLD, OLD, STORY

Here stands a tree with branches bowed to thee,
covered with your shades of glory, branches
bowed to tell your story!
You give us and our life worth: you let us serve
you on this earth!
We need to bow our head, as in your service
your word spread!
As you cover us with glory, help us to tell your
old, old, story!

WIDE ANGLE

The view so wide even your imagination has to stretch to get it all in. It is God showing just a little of his glory, in this, his created universe.

Colors, shapes, sizes, and variety reminding us of an awesome God! The scene where more earth and sky meet, more space and change can be seen than almost any other place on the face of this planet of ours!

Before us, around us, seeming to be apart of us! "Grand," indeed. A canyon "indeed," truly A Grand Canyon!!!

27

LONELY TABLE

The picnic table sits empty
now in the growing shade of a
lovely spring day. The leaves give
energy to the trees as they come
forth in the warm spring
sunshine.

The lake near by shimmers as
it too reflects the warmth of the
sun.

The rhythmical lapping of its
waves mesmerizes the viewer
with the peace of it all!

Soon that table, empty now,
will receive the many visitors of
the season, offering the comfort
and convenience
of its bench seats and table top.

Children will laugh and run
off to play rather than finish
their meal. Young folks will
share romantic smiles as they
share a quiet lunch.
Those of us who have been the
child or the young starry-eyed or
part of the family outing
are now here just to sit and share
memories and enjoy the lunch
prepared by our lives!

The table will be well used;
people will leave their marks;
and if the table could talk, what
stories it could tell!!

But for now, the table sits at
rest in anticipation, quiet, empty,
and alone among the trees that
provide its home!

SNOW TREES

*My gnarled age in winters sleep, praying,
to our Lord my life to keep!*

The evergreen family of trees!

The Eagle Witness

I saw this bird sitting high in a tree, on top of the world it seemed to me.

Poised in a regal stance, looking like royalty and not by chance.

Head crowned in white, its beak showing power, yet having grace and beauty like a lovely flower.

There that eagle stood not saying a word, yet sending a message everyone heard.

"I am the master, ruler of the skies! Listen, hear me, for I am wise.

"There is one other, the true master and king, who loves us and let's us do our thing!

"It is His love and grace that gives us life; His goodness and mercy that takes away our strife.

"All honor and praise is His due. Be sure that it comes, comes from you.

"Serve our master, Christ the Lord. Truly in serving you will never be bored.

"The Lord will know that you have tried, and in His house you will, in the end, abide!"

COLOR OF PROMISE

After the waters had covered the earth and

the people left realized their worth,

God showed his colors to us from the sky,

a reminder to all of the wherefore and why.

The colors of promise is that rainbow bright

remains forever a glorious sight.

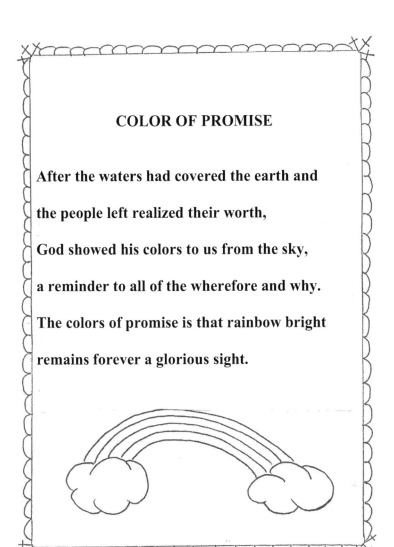

HATCHING LIFE

*The nest was made; the eggs were laid; mother
hen had started her event!!*

*She sat real proud, then clucked out loud, "Look
what the Lord has sent"*

*The warmth of her breast on the nest soon gave
movement to the eggs!*

*A wing, a feather, no matter the weather, came
first the head or legs.*

*That blessed event that God had sent broke forth
from the womb of a shell.*

*Bobbing and chirping, even urping, so you knew
that all was well.*

*Soft and warm for a chick, that's norm. The
little ones scampered about.*

*Downy, not frowny, and full of life, mother hen
was heard to shout,*

*"See what I've done! See what fun my family now
seems to enjoy,*

*"Now all that I see, I hope you agree to let them
grow up, I employ!*

*"For old age to take them, and then only when they
have lived their life full.*

*That these baby chicks have gotten their kicks
and have done all the tricks they could pull!"*

32

AN "OLD SMOOTHIE"

An old smoothie is something or someone that works well without friction; a well crafted piece of furniture or a finely tooled machine, working well, serving a long time with a minimum of wear and tear.

I like to think of the love of my life as my old smoothie. We do work well together, and if there is ever a hint of friction, we oil it with an added dose of love and understanding!

We are crafted as a fine pair that really fit well together , and our sewing gives each other better, longer lasting life with a minimum of wear and tear!

We are a pair of old smoothies fitting side by side in life, wearing so well on each other!

Thank God for His craftsmanship! Amen!

ICE COVERED FINGERS

Fields of large bony hands with ice- covered fingers reaching out to the sun, melt me, melt me, as the fingers bend under the weight. The sun glistens, forming the shimmering silver outreach.
Slowly the beauty drips from the limbs, and the bare empty fingers prepare for the summer growth of the beauty green!

LONELY CLOUD

There was a lonely cloud in the clear blue sky,
just floating around not knowing why!
The sky is so blue and clear and true, that
the little cloud didn't know what to do.
He floated all around feeling God's sun, wondering
why he was the only one.
So he told the good Lord that he was bored and
he wanted a family, too.
So the Lord looked around and finally found other
clouds in the sky.
He put them together and changed the weather, and
the earth turned green by and by!
So if you're lonely and just floating around, talk to
our Lord .He is there to be found!
He'll put you together with someone, too, so you'll
change the weather in all you do!!

MARVELOUS THINGS

DAUGHTERS

One for the money, two for show!
I have two daughters don't you know!

Life is filled with marvelous things!
Daughters fair; I have a pair filled with warmth
and charm and a love so rare!
With love by my side, these two are my pride,
sharing and caring as the Lord is their guide.
The frills of their youth and visions of gentle
play, now replaced by their own family's every day!
To me they are still children soft and sweet,
filling my life with all things neat!

Love Dad, "Don't let the bugs bite!"

FIREFIGHTERS

Life is filled with marvelous things when heroes need to be born!

The sirens sounded, and bells did ring. I jumped into my gear ready to do my thing!

In record time we jumped on board as the driver shouted "Ready" and off we roared.

We raced through the streets with sirens and lights ablaze. As firefighters all the citizens we did amaze!

Reaching the fire, acting like a team, prepared and ready for that fire, we were mean!

All together with hoses drawn, we advanced fearlessly up the lawn!

A cry upstairs could soon be heard, so up went the ladder without a word.

Hoses were out; the water was spraying; I saw one of the neighbors. I thought she was praying!

Reaching the window, we found a mother and child. The crowd below was almost going wild!

Flames went higher, almost licking their feet. The firemen could surely feel the heat.

Then grabbing the child from the mothers arms, we took her down the ladder, away from harm!

The hoses and men who challenged that fire were beginning to win in their fighting attire.

The mother too, came safely down to the cheers of what seemed like the whole darn town!

The flames did burn some memories away, but a little girl and her mom had another day!

"You are heroes," they said in the paper, the next day, "We were just doing our job! We liked it that way!"

RADIO

Life is filled with marvelous things.

Young men, especially when they get to be 12 or 13 years old, really think they can do almost anything. Their imaginations are wonderful, and there is no end to their curiosity!

There were special times in the evening when I would have "charge" of the radio in the living room. It was a time when I felt all powerful and in control as I sat in front of that big Coronado radio with the green eye.

I took that knob in my hand, turning ever so carefully watching that green eye, one way, then the other, till the eye came as close together as possible. That fine tuning meant that the AM station with my favorite programs would "come in," so I could listen: Jack Armstrong, Sky King, The Shadow, Buck Rogers, Inner Sanctum, The Green Hornet, Superman, and more!

It was a marvelous world of imagination and make believe as I listened, watched the green eye on the radio and became transported to a different time and place. Many pleasant evenings were spent in front of that radio, many hours of using my mind's eye to "see" stories, plots, and adventures, unfold!

The mind is a marvelous thing. Challenged by sight or sound or whatever, it can create, invent, solve, and serve its owner, never leaving one bored!!

ROAMING

Life is filled with marvelous things like candy, good buddies, and bee stings!

One sunny day in the month after May, my buddies and I went for a walk.

We all took candy, thought that was dandy, then proceeded to walk and talk!

Our dreams, it seems, were fantasies for sure, as we all searched for our boredom cure,

trips to the moon, really soon, and a car that would run on air.

Peace in our time would be fine and cures for ills we thought unfair,

solving all problems of time and space and becoming a real space ace.

But as it often does, it's the common that came first, like running out of candy and getting home late; that's worse!

So we made our about face and went back to the place, from which we started to roam,

back to security, comfort, and warmth, love from our family, the place we call home!

PUDDLE

Life is filled with marvelous things, especially after a rain.

The summer shower was over; the sun was coming out; and looking around the yard, there were puddles all about.

One little puddle, just being there, looked so inviting to me! It crossed my mind that I had to find how deep that it could be!

It never matters what you wear, if they're Sunday best or everyday. You're going to run and jump right in that puddle anyway!

Oh, what fun to see the splash, all that water fly about, until you heard your mother's voice as she began to shout!

"Get out of that water. What's the matter with you. Don't you know any better?" I guess I might if I had thought, but for now I'd just get wetter!

Out of the house, her arms in the air, "What is a mother to do? I try to teach, to do my best, to understand and be patient with you.

"But it matters not, like some dark plot. You're determined to have it your way!

"Live and learn; it's hard to discern, when we give one advice every day.

"If children really listen, or even care, when we do our very best to teach,

"To help, to guide, to support with pride, till someday old age they'll reach."

When so many of life's puddles will have long since gone away,

Leaving a boring dry yard and no puddle in which to play!

If this has happened and that's where you are, go outside after a rain. Look for the biggest, most tempting puddle and jump. You only have fun to gain!!!!!

MY WAGON

Life is filled with marvelous things.

Some of my earliest memories as a child come to me when I was about 3 or 4 years old. I remember living in a house at the top of a big hill on the north end of town. It was a big hill.

The house was white stucco and had hollyhocks, that mother cared for around it, and other stuff. I remember it had a front porch all across the front that I played on. One day when my older cousin and his mom came, we were playing on that porch. My cousin climbed up on a stool, fell down, and broke his arm. I was too young to feel real bad but remember he had his arm tied up for some time after, and it was harder to play with him.

I've always liked to go places even at that early age. Now I really don't remember why any more, but one day I decided to run away! I remember mom telling me what to do, dressing me in silly clothes like a sailor suit and telling me not to get dirty "Be careful. Don't go anywhere!" Maybe that was enough! I had had it!

I had a little red wagon that Mom used to set me in and pull me around. I used it to play with when at home. I would haul "stuff" around.

"On this one day at this one time, I did a marvelous thing. I ran away from home, but I did not go alone! Mother caught up with me at the bottom of the hill. I had a handkerchief on a stick over my shoulder, and I was pulling my wagon!

I remember pulling that wagon and "stuff" up that hill was harder than bringing it down. I remember it was a little harder to sit down, too for a while after I got home.

I remember those lessons learned all my life and I'm grateful! That wagon is long since gone, but I've never forgotten what it was like to pull that "stuff" around!!

CAPTAIN, OH CAPTAIN!

The boat gently bobbed as it held firmly to the dock, tied by its owner left around the clock!

Ready to serve when its owner was near, to fish or to cruise, it held all the gear!

The owner did come with friends or alone. When untied from the dock, the boat's power was shown,

Out over the water, leaving a foamy white wake, responding to all commands, making no mistake.

With the wind in his face and a resolute smile, the owner'd rush to "his spot" to fish awhile.

This captain of the seas felt the sun and the breeze, surrounding his kingdom, bringing all others to their knees!

It mattered not if he had not caught a fish or got even a bite. He is the captain of his world, ruler of all, and that's just out of sight!

The warm sun fades and shadows form. It's time to get back and return to norm.

The captain of the sea, that would be me, returns to tie up his boat!

"Where have you been? I don't know when you're ever on time, you old goat!"

Reality does come to everyone when things get a little late, but never fear for this old dear, for with his boat he has another date!

FLYING

Life is filled with marvelous things when you're looking for something to do!

I sat on the back steps, head in my hand, with a far-off look in my eye.

My mind wandered; my eyes wondered as I looked at some birds in the sky.

Why can't I fly like that bird in the sky and look down on the people below?

Just raise my arms while I leave the ground and give all below a show?

Let them be amazed as I soar through the sky, high as the clouds above,

Dipping and turning with the ease of a bird flying, as if you were in love.

But pop goes the dream as Mother's voice is heard, back down to earth. It took only one word!

REALITY

Life is filled with marvelous things!

I sometimes feel that life is unreal, that what happens just cannot be,

That I'm the only one things happen to, and why does it have to be me?

How foolish it is to mark myself and to think I'm the only one

Who's put up with torments and temptations and people making fun.

I need only remember God's son who died to set us free,

Who took it all; it was His call. He did it for you and me!

Life is real, God's gift to us. We need to serve and not make a fuss!

QUIET POWER

Life is filled with marvelous things, some of which we cannot see!

But just because we cannot see or taste or touch, does not mean they cannot be.

The power of the wind that fills the sails moving boats and great ships along,

The feeling of joy and peace with love, filling your heart with song,

The warmth of a fire in cold weather or just being together with someone to touch,

Are things unseen that happen to all that affects our lives so much,

forces that move our bodies and lives around, moving our minds without a sound.

We need only accept and keep the faith and in our lives God's love will abound.

For the greatest unseen source of power and given by Gods command,

Is prayer, to be sure, to help us endure, as long as we do not demand!

Our Lord in His grace will help us in our place and be with us every step of the way!

His promise is sure: we shall endure, and He will be there every day!

LIFE IS FILLED

Life is filled with marvelous things if we only stop and think.

There are times we feel that life is filled only with problems, and perhaps at times it is, but they are only problems if we let them be; and they fill our life only if we do not let God into our lives to help us.

It is very easy to nurture a problem, to point the finger, to blame someone or something, to say and let yourself believe that you can do nothing to change!

It is not like we are the only ones that have problems; we all do! The difference is what we do with them!

I have never been able to handle a problem on my own; no one can. We try; we do our best; we even seem to solve some of them and move on; but only God can understand and forgive a problem! Only our Lord can give us the strength we need to carry on!

There will always be problems, but to each problem there will always be help and forgiveness if we only ask and believe. We do have choices!

May the Lord and giver of life surround you in your life,
May He help and strengthen you through all your strife.
May He give and forgive and fill your life with peace,
so that in your life you will have a new lease!

AMEN!

ANGEL IN THE GLASS

Life is filled with marvelous things!
On a counter top in my home is a snifter glass
all alone!
Inside that glass an angel does stand,
with harp in hand looking so grand!
One can almost hear heavenly music play,
as I watch that angel every day!
Standing tall, strumming the notes, as from
that harp heavenly music floats!
A gentle scene that inspires my soul,
to make heavenly music my goal!
I imagine myself in God's heavenly choir,
singing His melodies to inspire!
Singing forever, how happy I would be to
sing for our Lord because He serves me!

TAKE YOUR AGE AND LOVE IT!

Life is filled with marvelous things; it's a challenge to remember them all!

When I was first born, I remember nothing really, but how wonderful it must have felt to be held in your parents' arms, to feel so warm and secure as they held you, carried you, rocked you, sang to you, and gave you all those hugs and kisses.

How satisfying and powerful it must have felt to get so much attention with a sigh or a smile or crying or even passing gas!

How good it must have felt inside and outside when you were fed and had your diaper changed! Ah, the good young days!

Life, it seems to me, offers different stages of control; every age has its own! When you're young, it's the crying or whining or having a fit that seems to work pretty well! Some people use these all their lives! Generally, as one matures, we develop other talents such as threats, even a gentle or not so gentle push, bite, or kick. Ganging up is good if there is a lot of territory involved.

Developing other talents and abilities that gain respect is a far better way to go. To train your young body and mind to accomplish good things, and to help and serve others brings back to oneself a satisfaction and power money cannot buy. Even at a young age, it is good to have someone give you a pat on the head and tell you that you are a good person. As you get older, you may receive a pat on the back, a certificate or perhaps even a testimonial, or maybe just a "thank you!" It could also be just your own feeling of self worth even, if no one else recognizes it!

We live with ourselves all our lives. It is important to get to know ourselves and find satisfaction if we ever hope to find a measure of happiness. Not everyone can climb Mt. Everest, sail around the world, or whatever. Your Mt. Everest might simply be owning your own home or having a loving family!

Age changes abilities; age changes goals; age changes most everything except who we really are!

It is, therefore, most important in our lives ,no matter where we are in our earth age, to be true to ourselves, to have faith, to live openly, to share honestly, to be generous with the blessings God has given us, and to love!

I love where I am now, youthful abilities and talents I no longer have, but I thank God I had them once and had the chance to use them!

This aging body can no longer perform the tasks of my youth, but I thank God I had my chance!

The mind, the eyes, the ears, all my senses, are showing signs of many years of use, and I can no longer see, hear, or remember as well as before, but thank God for all that I have seen and heard. Thank God that even now I can, in my own way, with the God-given talents and abilities I still have, I can live my life to the fullest!

Thank God I can still love and be loved!

TINKER BELLS AND TELEPHONE RINGS

Life is filled with marvelous things like tinker bells and telephone rings!

My youngest daughter's household has a large loveable cat.

I like that cat, cause it acts like a dog; and you usually know where it's at!

That loveable cat is called Tinker Bell. She doesn't listen though she knows her name well!

But she'll stay by your side and look at you with pride. Her devotion is not a hard sell.

Now the telephone that rings can mean many things. It can be good or bad!

I like it best for the opportunities it brings every time the darn thing rings!

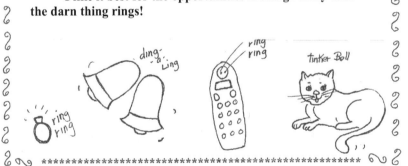

WEATHER OR NOT!

MELODY OF RAIN

In the still of the evening after sun set, I felt a few drops; I was getting wet!

The quiet pitter-patter of the gentle drops, was music to those who had planted crops.
The music swelled to a crescendo of sound, a symphony of moisture as it hit the ground!
Life springs forth as God gives us rain, sent to nourish our crops so we all may gain!

WHEN THE WIND BLOWS

Summer's end is coming near; soon on the calendar autumn will appear!

Not to fret, not to worry, as all summer projects end in a flurry.

Life too, has a summer's end; it is our prayer, it ends as a friend!

Autumn winds are bolder now, more crisp and challenging somehow.

The crispness adds to summer's end with the challenge that autumn, too, should be your friend.

Autumn in life means a fresh start for us to proceed and in a full life take part!

Winter winds can blow hard and cold; they can make you feel you are getting old!

But winter, too, has a beauty all its own, with the pure white in its snow that's blown!

All seasons' winds blow constant change. We need to remember that God our lives did arrange!

For after the winter, spring begins and eternal life that never ends!

Thank you, Lord, for Your winds of love, for all Your grace and mercy from above!

EVERY SEASON HAS A REASON!

White webs of snow cover the bare limbs of the winter trees where in the summer, green leaves did cover.

Now covered in soft pure snow, the tree rests.

Winter's beauty of white is shared by more than just the trees.

Our eyes are filled with wonderful shades and shadows of white everywhere we look, accented by occasional summer color that peeks through. There is beauty everywhere!

Winter's rainbow, the evergreen, is there to remind us that life continues all year, that new life will be shared again as spring comes and the resting trees and plants again show their beauty in color to the world.

Life has it's "Seasons," times to grow, to develop, to mature, to gently age, and rest. Our "rainbow, "our "Evergreen," is the Christ Child born in a manger, our promise of eternal life where we shall forever grow in the grace and presence of our Heavenly Father.

Praise God for life's seasons, and whichever one we are in, remember there will always be another, the eternal gift from our Lord!

Praise God, Amen

THERE IS REASON IN THE SEASON

This is the season! What season? Why it's Christmas, of course!

Is Christmas just another season to us? A time of the year that provides some changes in weather and attitude?

Perhaps in calling it a "season" we expect only that it is a time of year that comes and goes.

Christmas is not a season, Christmas is a "reason;" a reason to remember God's greatest gift, a reason to honor and praise, to worship, to give thanks to our God, the Father, for that gift!

The Christmas "reason" is all life long. The Christmas reason is to be celebrated all life long. The Christmas reason does not come and go; nor will it ever change!

The Christmas reason has changed us, changed our lives!

Let this "Earthly Christmas Season" become our Christmas "reason" to honor, to praise, to worship, and to give thanks to our Heavenly Father every day of our lives.

We have been given a blessed Christmas reason. May we share that gift with all we meet and bring true joy to the world!!

NEW YEAR'S EVE

It is the eve of a new calendar year—party time!

Is celebrating the new calendar year really so important?

Make your resolutions; rethink the past year; set your goals for the New Year; resolve old problems; start anew, fresh.

Out with the old. In with the new, and we toast it all night long!

Life is not one big party. The eve of a new calendar year is not the only time one needs to get rid of the old and start anew.

Every evening in life is time to rethink the day, to make resolutions, to set new goals, to try to resolve old problems.

Thank the Lord that He has given you that day, and ask His forgiveness for your mistakes. Ask Him for a good full night's rest that you may begin fresh in a new day. The only toast you need is from the toaster for your breakfast!

I would wish you each day "a happy new day." May it be filled with the presence of God in your life. God will, in his time, resolve all your old problems, and in his time, give you the only goal you need, if only you have faith and believe!

May our Lord guide you each new day!

May He keep you always along His way!

HAPPY "NEW DAYS" IN THE NEW YEAR!

January					
1	2	3	4	5	6
7	8	9	10	11	12	13
14	15	16	17	18	19	20
21	22	23	24	25	26	27
28	29	30	31			

DRIFTS

Together with friends, the wind included, they gather in drifts in places precluded.

Growing, shifting, like an evening tide, sometimes Narrow, sometimes wide.

Flowing like an overflow, always changing, and on the go!

Drifting changes the earth as we know it, giving inspiration to the words of this poet.

So drift, shift, and change at will. Your spirit and beauty will move us still!!!

SNOW FLAKES

A snow flake falls; not a sound is heard; another, yet
Another; they say not a word.

Their beauty began as droplets in the sky, moisture
formed high till on the ground they lie.

Gathering together, a white blanket they form, changing
the appearance of summer's norm.

Winter supports their beauty now, causing some the
need to plow.

Snowflakes so small , yet growing tall, changing our
lives till spring comes to call.

63

RAIN PLUS

I heard the rain and it comforted me, the drops were soothing to the touch, ever so gentle yet sometimes hard but always welcome.

God is after all the master gardener, His rain nourishes the soil and our crops grow. The trees, shrubs, flowers all receive life from each drop. All plants have purpose even those we may not like. God sends the rain for all.

After the rain comes Gods rainbow promise, the sun also shines on all, and receives its power. Plants, animals, human, all living things, God cares for us.

Lest it be to easy He also sends trials to help us to remember and appreciate those blessings we do have! Thank God for it all!

Let the rain wet our minds that they may grow peaceful thoughts. Let the sun give us the energy to share that peace! Amen

Shhh!

HUSH

There was a hush surrounding me as I sat in God's silent wonderland. The beauty of God's frozen breath on the trees, provided moving highlights and shadows as the sun shown through them!

The scene was one that brought a hush to a busy day, peace to a restless soul!

A gentle breeze stirred as God came by. You could feel His presence!

This quiet hush was broken only by the distant sounds of motor vehicles as they carried passengers to their destinations.

The snow, all the snow, resting where it had fallen and where others had, shoveled, pushed, plowed or blown it into huge piles, covering the earth like a giant white filter, a filter between the dirt of the earth and the purity of the sky. Will it ever melt away?

For now the snow adds to the hush, a pure muffler of white flakes absorbing the sounds around!

This winter vision is providing and sharing the beauty of God's creation in temperatures that preserve the snow, nevertheless, enter and leave the heart with a warm, peaceful "hush."

FIRESIDE

It was just a hint of crispness that filled the air, with a reminder and a promise of what was yet to come.

The lush green leaves are paler now after a summer of work and a job well done. Growth has happened; trees have shared their shade; plants have blossomed; kids have sold lemonade.

The den inside has more attraction now, the comfort of my favorite chair, the carved oak mantel, the old iron grate with a birch log lying there. A match, a light, a flame that begins to grow, flickering at first, then fully becoming quite a show, giving more than warmth and the beauty of the flame, giving comfort and peace; nothing else is quite the same!

To relax and enjoy the warm show and glow is to savor each moment and never want to go.

My fireside chair and the time spent there have values rich as coins so rare!

Comfort, serenity, and peace are all mine. My kingdom, my life and my future are all fine!

HEAVEN OPENS

Snow falls gently on the earth below. God opens His heaven to share the pure white of His salvation!

His love covers our land with a blanket of caring, giving beauty to bare shapes of ugly.

Winter comes to life also, but so does our Lord's love! He continues to cover our "shapes of whatever" with His blanket of white mercy and forgiveness!

God cares for us through all seasons, through all the years of our life, and God will make us beautiful with His snow of love.

Thank You, Lord, for opening Your heavens to us to share the beauty of Your love with all you have created. Thank You for sharing it with me. Amen!

RAIN

The grass was crisp, the flowers did droop; the yard did need some of God's "Chicken soup!"

The sun shone bright with all its might, starting in the morning until it was night!

We do like the sun, as most everyone, but after too much, it did lose its fun!

The gathering clouds promised a change. It is something that our Lord did arrange.

A drop here and there and then with a flair, it came down hard causing people to stare!

The crispness was gone, the dryness broken; many kind words from growers were now spoken!

All settled in and with a slight grin, felt a great comfort of warmth within.

The rain turned gentle and a lot more kind as it gave all the people a great peace of mind!

LIFE'S ACCEPTANCE

Life seems such a mess at times, having no reasons or rhymes!

It's then we should remember that You care and will guard and protect us anywhere.

We need only put our trust in Thee and accept Thy offer of eternity!

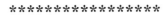

PEACE

Peace comes when your mind settles down.
Peace comes when there's quiet in the heart.
Peace comes when your cares fade into the background.
Peace comes when the roar of life becomes a whisper.
Peace comes when the good Lord takes over.
Peace comes when you let Him!
Peace!

****

FALL

The bold, cold winds force the remaining leaves off the trees, pushing and shoving the warm summer days out of the way.

The rule of fall is everywhere in the briskness of each day.

Even the sun has lost its warm orange edge, replaced by the cooler soft yellows.

The seasons change, each bringing its own special weather that tells all just what it is!

TALKS TO GOD!

PEACE

Peace can be elusive, very hard to find, playing all sorts of tricks on our mind!

If we search too hard, it will not be found; we need to relax to let peace abound.

To remember and believe that God gives us peace, is to open troubled hearts and give life a new lease!

"To accept and listen to God's holy word" no better advice will ever be heard.

May the peace of God fill your days with warmth and love and happiness always!

LOVE SURROUNDS US

God's love surrounds us as we live our lives. We wake in the morning to the warmth of His love, as our day begins. If we are blessed we may share that love with someone we meet; if we are further blessed we may share that love with the love of our life!

Our Lord shows His love blessing us with our lives, with his forgiveness, with His grace and mercy as He supports us with His presence through all of life's problems!

With our faith we accept, with our faith we give thanks, with our faith God leads us to eternal life.

With our faith we will share our eternal life with those we have loved in this earthly life!

God's love knows no end; our love will never end; the memories of this life and the sharing of our love will never end!

Thank the Lord for His love, as He shares that love from heaven above!

Thank the Lord for our love, that we have shared and risen above!

Thank the Lord, for He will always be the personal savior of you and me!

BLESSINGS

When we wrap all things together, when
we think all the thoughts, do all the deeds we
must realize that it is God after all that gives
us, by His grace, blessings. Try as we may to
say we worked for, we accomplished, we earned,
we did it all, it is God who has given us His
blessings out of His goodness and mercy. It is
God who gives us our life, our talents, our
abilities to use in His service. This is most
certainly true, this we must certainly do. Amen

75

POWER?

Strength comes from muscles. Where does power come from? What is power?

Muscles can, of course, give a kind of power. Fear can have a kind of power! Wealth and/or position can have a kind of power. The physical size of a person or the words someone uses can have a kind of power!

For the most part, a lot of the power we recognize comes from some kind of fear!

I would suggest to you that true power , the most powerful power, comes not from muscles or fear but from respect!

Respecting someone enough to believe in them, to follow and to do what they ask. When someone has that kind of power that person must never betray those virtues that have earned that power!

The power of one born some 2,000 years ago is such a power!

When we fear and love God, it is not because we are afraid but because we truly love and respect what He has done and continues to do for us; Never to betray us, never to let us go, always there to guide us, to give us the strength we need, and to forgive our sins!

God's offer through his grace is eternal life, if only we believe and ask for it. God has the power to grant it!

I NEED THE LORD ALMIGHTY

I   -And so it is in "this" world, that in the beginning and in the end, it is "I" I am closer to me than anyone; I feel I know me better than anyone; I am the only one who can do what I do or think what I think. I am important!

NEED   -And so it is that I, being so important, have needs. I need guidance, strength, and wisdom. I need help in my life from beginning to end because I am important!

THE   -And so it is, that in being important and needing; that I get it from "the" best place!

LORD   -And so it is, that my importance, my needs are met by "the" best source, the Lord. From my beginning, which the Lord, by his grace created, through my life that He has valued important enough to send His Son to take away my sins. The Lord through His life Has as given my life value!

ALMIGHTY   -And so my important, valuable life, my need of forgiveness and guidance in my life, the very presence of the Lord in my life, is my command, my inspiration, my desire to serve my Lord, the almighty one that rules over all. He is almighty in power, almighty in grace, almighty in mercy, almighty in forgiveness, and almighty in His offer of eternal life-if we have faith and believe!

Thank you, Almighty Lord!

TRUE PICTURE

There is a mist in the air. It's beginning to gather on the windshield distorting the visions of the outside world.

Yet here I sit within the comfort of my automobile, in a park of my youth. Memories all around that seem so clear inside the car are becoming a blur, requiring more and more imagination on the outside.

Life can be so clear on the inside and so distorted on the outside. We need to remember where we really are!

The place we're in may be filled with wonderful memories of a time gone by; but the here and now, even in the same place, are different; and so are we.

Water has been going over that dam for as long as I can remember, the same dam, different water.

I have been opening my eyes to another day for a long time, each just 24 hours, yet brand new and different.

Life needs to move on even as water over the dam moves downstream affecting its banks all along the way, sometimes flooding, washing away "stuff" along its path, sometimes leaving a rich deposit of earth where things may grow!

I know that in my life I have picked up my share of "stuff" and carried it along only to dump it somewhere else along the way. I pray that I have also been able to leave deposits of good thoughts and actions that may grow and nourish a new generation!

Lord, help me wash out the junk in my life.
Help me carry away those things that cause strife.
Let me leave deposits of inspiration and hope,
so that with life, others may cope.
Thank you, Lord, for letting my life flow
And for your promise of eternal life where I can go!

THE ENDLESS MIND

Sometimes when my eyes are raised to the heavens; and I recall astronomers telling of all that is up there; time, space, and numbers that seem almost endless, I reflect on the mind!

I marvel often at my own mind and all the curiosity, questions, decisions and problems that my own thought process gets me into, these, too, seem endless.

I make no claims that I have an exceptional mind. Indeed, I thank God that I am not exceptional; those minds must be unstable whirlwinds of activity. As it is, I cannot seem to ease my own, to lull myself into a relaxed mode when the "hurt" of activity cries out for peace. Fortunes are made on headache pills, etc.. Not that I take pills for my headaches. Thank God I have not for some years; that's why I know my mind is endless!

If all we do is think of our problems, we create even more; and there will be no ends to those either, no end because we have imposed a limit on our minds.

We must give the Good Lord credit and use our minds to think through the problems, think right on past them. We do have choices; God will help us with His solution!

God will give us the strength to accept and the wisdom not to try to understand, for trying to understand would only add to the problems.

I thank God for my endless mind that has given me faith to use my endless mind. Amen.

OPEN ME LORD

My sky seems dark, at least gray most of the time!
I long for the sunshine!

The gray and the darkness are beginning to wear like a long winter. I yearn for spring!

Clouds of problems are keeping out the sun; the night of troubles seems endless.

I look at the forecast through my eyes, and the winter is not going away. The clouds never seem to part. Each day is the same!

I seem to be open only to the troubles and problems of this world.

I had better take another look at the forecast!
God never promised us a total blue sky
or constant blessings.

His total and constant presence is His pledge.

This is more than enough to give our life an edge.

For clouds of problems and troubles that seem endless.

God, as our Savior and friend, takes all our "stuff" with no end, changes the dark, and changes the gray for us into a bright new day.

Are not problems or troubles all because we are not friendless?

Thank you, Lord, please open my life.
Yours is the forecast to end all strife.

Amen.

GENTLE LORD

Gentle Lord, as you hold me close, I can feel your arms around me
answering my prayer, always being there, your blessings in all that I see!
Guide my path and give me strength to live my whole life through
that I may serve and give you thanks for all the things You do!

THE VISIT

I had a visit with my Lord today.
He has helped me with His love along my life's way!
He gives me strength and courage, too.
He even sent His son, my sins to atone!
He has promised eternal life with Him, life in His
*   heaven that is free from sin!*
Thank you, Lord, for your blessings every day!
Thank you, Lord, for your help along my way!

"I SAW CHRIST"

Morning came early after a restless night. I opened
my eyes to the cold gray of my room. As I looked around
at the emptiness I felt the slight chill of the air, stimulating
my mind, reminding me that I was at the beginning of
another day.

Another day - Is every day just another day? Or is it
another opportunity for a Christ sighting for service to our
Lord to witness our Christ sightings, to help and serve those
around us?

I saw Christ today as soon as I opened my eyes. I saw
Christ in the cold gray of my room reaching out His hand
and telling me to get up! "I have given this new day to you.
Use it!"

I saw Christ in the warm clothes I was able to put on and
the breakfast I ate. I saw Christ in the phone call, in the car
I drove to be here where I can share His word with my peers.

I see Christ and His blessings filling my life!

I thank the Lord that I can see!

I pray that I am what He wants me to be.

In Thy Name I Pray, Amen.

 **AGE**

Age is the open door to life. Walk through it with joy in your heart!

God opens our door at birth; God gives us the key at baptism; God gives us His bible as our guide book.

Each day of our walk is a" blessing", Thank God!!

As mortals we create celebrations, one of which is our birthday, our own personal Christmas.

Each year on the anniversary of our birth we remind one and all we made it through another year. Presents and congratulations would be nice.

We look at the birthday person, smile, sing, spank, or whatever, perhaps a toast. Presents are opened, memories shared, everyone is happy, and then the party is over; but not really. A birthday happens every day we open our eyes on this old earth, and God presents us with a new day.

Although we may not feel like celebrating some days when adversities come along, we need only use God's guide book, the Bible, and remember His promise to always be there for us.

God saves the greatest gift of all when our birthdays on this earth are over!! God has promised eternal life with Him because of His birth, death and rising again. We will be able to celebrate His presence through all eternity!

Happy Birthday today and always! !
God loves you, and so do we!

NUMBER VALUES

1, 10, 1

The value of one is more than ten, if "you" happen to be that one.

The many mistakes we seem to make have all been forgiven by "one"!

Take all the numbers and add them up; they will never be greater than the Holy "One"!!

Add all of our sins, all of our gifts, all of our blessings, and thank the "one" who has given and forgiven and done it all for you!!

****

GOD'S TURN

The sky turns gray; the clouds have their way; the edge is gone from the day.

The sky wonders why, trying not to be shy, wants to give the sun another try!

The clouds now part. The sun has a new start. Oh, Lord, How Great Thou Art!!

PURPOSE

Purpose should rule the world. Would that be so hard to take? We must only assume that the purpose be for the good and understand that what may be good for me may not be good for someone else. The good for someone else must be good for all!

Applied to anything, 'good' purpose should rule the world!

****

MOVING AHEAD

When your world is just not right, in fact, it is just out of sight,

Open yourself up and you will find that it can be "No, never mind."

In that openness you will see all of the possibilities that there can be.

Then moving ahead without looking behind, a kinder, gentler future you will find.

The past can haunt; it's full of strife. We must learn to get on with our life.

God is the answer; His forgiveness is there; it will help us all to go anywhere!

Take that forgiveness right to your heart. It will most assuredly give you a new start!

****

Reach for your future; do not put your future on hold! Do something! Do it now and make your movement bold!

STORIES OF YOUTH

LITTLE FLOW

I ran, as a boy, in fields with joy and places
where streams did flow!
I looked for a brook in some forest nook, as a
place I wanted to go!
It was neat on my feet as I took a seat on the
bank where the cool water did play!
It felt so good as I knew it would, particularly
on a hot summer's day.
Water bugs, tadpoles, and crayfish abound. I
think it was their heaven I found!
I watched them play; it made my day, until the
time for me to be homeward bound!
Rippling water, gently flow. That was the
place I wanted to go!

TREE IN THE MEADOW

There is a tree in the meadow all alone
sharing its shade with a friend.

A young doe on a warm sunny day looking
for someone its shade to lend!

So the doe and the tree shared their
space, putting a smile on a small child's
face!

"Look there, dad, see what I see! What
a great picture for just you and me!"

THE SANDBOX

There was a box in my backyard; it was a kingdom all its own,
Where kids did play all the day. Their loyalty to that box was shown!
A glorious kingdom filled with endless possibilities and dreams yet unborn!
Where anything could be built and often was, and spirits were never forlorn.
Move this here; pile that there and form the magic castle, where subjects listened and did their jobs, all without a hassle!
What marvelous kingdoms we did create with nothing else but sand!

THE BIKE!

Life is filled with marvelous things; and when you are young, they are wondrous as well.

When I was a child, before my teens, my parents did all they could for me. They gave me things money could not buy such as love, family, and a home! I was a "rich lad!"

Money was something else in those days; and when I wanted a bike, there were no funds in our budget for it.

I felt I was not a child but a young man even though I was only about 9 or 10, and I deserved a bike. All reasoning went for naught as there simply was not enough money!

I could earn it, Mom and Dad said, and I did try, whatever odd jobs a 9 year old could do.

In our town there was one theater that would give away prizes on a Saturday afternoon, such as bikes or even a motor scooter or two. The prizes were given away by drawing tickets given by merchants during the week.

Now Dad, bless his heart, always stopped at this one gas station where they gave tickets, and then he would bring them home.

One Saturday afternoon Dad gave me a nickel, and Mother arranged for me to go to the movie with my older cousin, who was our neighbor. Mother also took all of Dads tickets, I think about six or eight, and put the numbers on a small sheet of paper that I took along with the tickets.

I don't remember what the movie was, but I do remember sitting in the middle of the theater, more toward the back!

Time came for the drawing; the whole place lit up; the manager and someone else came on the stage! There was some kind of drum with a door on it that they turned over and over.

There was also the most beautiful bike in the world, a SPEED-O-KING, with white wall tires, a carrier on the back, a horn in a case on the frame, a chain guard, a light on the handlebars, and the most beautiful paint job!!

Some numbers were called for smaller prizes; then came the BIKE!! I was holding my paper from Mom, with the numbers on it as best a 9 year-old could. Then I heard the number! My young eyes looked at the numbers on the paper, I thought I saw it! They called again -1 poked my cousin and pointed as I was unable to make a sound! Before the number was called the third time, my cousin poked me; and I said something, I'm not sure what!!

My older cousin took my hand, and the two of us took the winning ticket up to the stage! I WON! I REALLY WON!

I did not know how to ride a bike. It was almost too big besides, but my cousin put me on the carrier and rode me home. What a sight!

My life and my horizons changed after that day. A new world opened up to explore. I found parks and streams and fields and woods. I could ride all over town and around, even out to the gravel pit to swim with the other "guys" and go other "places."

I used it to go to school, to jobs, even to other towns as I got a little older.

I still have that bike, close to 60 years old now, with most of the original parts. Most of all I have my memories of a time when the value of that bike meant all the world to me. When learning how to ride it, I put some scratches on; but they never kept me from getting around. Through the snow in the winter delivering papers, or in the rain to school or work; it has always been a faithful friend!

My life is something like that bike. I started out all shiny and new, got a few scratches along the way, but always hung in there. I fixed my flat tires, kept my chain and brakes repaired. I've modified my frame a little but I'm good for a few more miles!

THE OPEN DOOR

There was an open door when I was a child, and out it I did go!

Too young to be afraid or care or remember my mother saying, "I told you so!"

Out I went happily into the sunshine, pulling my little red wagon!

No thoughts or fears or anxieties, just out to kill the dragon!

A knight was I, on my own special quest!

I meant to get that dragon; I did not jest!

I had no horse, but that did not matter!

I heard my red wagon's wheels. How they did clatter!

Over the gravel driveway and on to the road,

My world got much bigger, and I got more bold!

Down the road and down the hill, red wagon firmly in tow.

Off on my own adventure with my imagination, I did go!

Then as suddenly as it started, through that open door,

My mother caught up with me and made part of me sore!

My adventure was over, the dragon never found!

Per chance when I get older, I'll have a second time around!

ONCE I PUT MY RIGHT SOCK ON FIRST!!!

We are indeed creatures of habit. Our life falls into patterns, predictable patterns.

It all begins at the beginning, the beginning of the day!

How do you wake up? Do you bounce out of bed when you first open your eyes? Is it an alarm that does the job, or do you wake up on your own at the same time every morning? Do you lie in bed and make excuses not to get up, or do you begin to plan your day?

Do you go to the bathroom first or get dressed first? Do you have your clothes laid out, or do you scramble for something to wear?

Do you finish grooming in the bathroom before or after breakfast? Do you go out or make your own? What do you make or where do you go?

Do you have a set time for each activity before going to work or is it just "get up and hurry?"

Regardless, I would imagine there is the same routine followed every morning. We live with it. We know what to expect, and we just settle in.

And so goes the day; work times, break times, lunch times, bathroom times, call times, meeting times, every thing in a time and place. Our life goes merrily on its routine way; even our times to complain and perhaps even the people we complain to are the same. We don't necessarily need to be happy, just not surprised.

Well, once I put my right sock on first, and I haven't been the same since!!!!

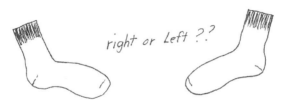

right or Left ??

95

CHILDLIKE MEMORIES

Somewhere there is a child in us just waiting to get out,
waiting ever patiently to get out and about,
to act the way we used to do without a second thought,
even though it may be something that we had not really
ought.

To throw away all present fears of what might happen
when, and just go out and do it, like we did then.
Oh carefree youth, with all its splendor, come back
now with memories so tender. For memories are what we
have, no matter what our age. Memories to fill our thoughts,
perhaps even slightly change.

The wonder of it all as time goes by, is our willingness to
share and not be quite so shy.
Remember well those early years and never let
them go, caress and share them so that others may know.

For all those memories good and bad are
what we leave, as our worth, when we pass and
meet our maker, when we leave this good old earth.

THE ANTS AND I

There was a boy with baggy pants who liked
to run and to play with ants.
Running was fun, and it didn't matter where
he would run. There was no record to shatter.
The ants, too, were fun to see. I often wished
their strength was in me!
Great loads they would carry much bigger by
far, than their small funny bodies are.
They would carry, and scurry all in a row,
following the leader who knew just where to go!
Together they would work from dawn to
dusk, storing their supplies; it was a must!
To be prepared, it seemed to me, just like the
Boy Scout I wanted to be!
I had much to learn and much to grow, much
experience before I would know how to succeed or
even try, how to understand and not wonder why!
The ants seemed to me to have a good plan.
They all worked together as should man.
Man could learn a lot from ants, to put aside
the "don'ts" and "can'ts."
To work together for the good of all, to not
give up but heed God's call!!

WINTER RISING

Eyes not yet open, the new day to see, the cold crisp air awakened me!

My body kept warm by sheep that had been shorn, but out from under I could see-

My breath like a mist; yet Mom did insist, "It's time to get up, now hurry!"

Hurry indeed! If I could succeed, I'd move so fast I'd be blurry!

Dress I did; I was a good kid. I paid attention to what Mom said!

I obeyed her call 'cause after all, she would have "helped" me get out of my bed.

Down in the kitchen the whole mood changed. The warmth of the stove did it all.

I knew each morning with breakfast arranged, that I'd always answer Mom's call!

BRRRRRR!

THE HILL

There is a hill far away where children go to play, to slide, to run, and all in all, just to have fun!

They gather on summer days with cheeks of tan. They gather on winter days whenever they can.

They rule the world on that hill, and if I were young, I would be there still!

THE COOL HOUSE OUTSIDE

The season was cold; I had to be bold and go to that cool house outside!

The urge was there; I did not care; I strolled down that path with pride!

I was old enough now not to start a row and walked the walk unafraid!

With my head held high I did not cry, I felt like I had it made!

I tried not to matter that my teeth did chatter, when I sat on that cold frosty seat!

I tried to grin, then hurried within to get back to the house and the heat!

When I came inside, I had my pride, all grown up I now thought!

But Mom knew and Dad did too, that complaining would go for naught!

MY WORLD FROM THE SIDEWALK STEP!

While growing up in my hometown I remember such marvelous things; as a sidewalk and the step! The sidewalk past our house was just a little lower than the walk to our house, so there we had a step.

I would watch the neighbors going to the corner store, or sending their reluctant kids. I would watch other kids both on my side of the street or across the street, playing on their sidewalks, roller skating, pulling wagons, pushing a two wheeled scooter, riding a trike or bike, or maybe playing hop-scotch, or other games, or perhaps, if no one was looking they would use the sidewalk for art work such as those hearts with two sets of initials inside them!

I could just sit and listen to the people talk as they went by; get to know them by their pleasant greetings and become true friends and neighbors!

If I listened carefully, I might hear which kid got into trouble; who had a new brother or sister; whose relative came to visit, or where they might be going on the weekend!

There was really no end to what I might learn just sitting quietly on my sidewalk step!

Now at certain times of the day the mailman would come by or the ice man and his truck filled with those big chunks of ice for the ice boxes. It was fun in the summer to run up, when the iceman went to deliver, to get a piece of good old "straight river ice" from the back of the truck and then suck on it until it was gone. Then there were other delivery trucks and even the paper boy that came by. I really admired that paperboy cause he was a little older and had to be real smart to remember where to deliver all those papers!

I would sit and watch the cars drive by on the street, why I could tell each make and model almost as soon as I would see them. I would wonder where they all were going, and make up stories about them.

I was never afraid to sit on my sidewalk step and my parents knew I was safe and out of the road! Sometimes they would sit on the front step of the house because their legs were longer and from there they would wave and talk to all those using the sidewalk.

As I grew older, sidewalks were places to meet during the day; maybe under the big shade tree on the corner of Oak and Main. There we would take care of the problems of the day; should we go to the woods? Should we make up a ballgame? Should we go swimming or what ever?

Then in the evening, as the sun slowly went down, the older boys and girls would meet, and the boys would "show off" and the girls would giggle. I thought someday I would be old enough to stay out past 9 o'clock and maybe even talk to a girl!

Well so much for that; I've grown up and many years have passed, but I must tell you there is still a part of me that is that little boy sitting on the sidewalk step.

Now I see places where people build houses and have no sidewalks, and I wonder how they can really call them neighborhoods.

Children play on the street with the traffic, and people out walking are out in the street with the traffic, and you know deep down in my heart I wish they could have a sidewalk step just like the one I had, just to sit on and watch the world go by; one to greet friends and neighbors; one for the kids to play on or just sit and watch and learn; a sidewalk to draw on, to ride on, to meet as I once did! I even used to get up on my two wheeled bike so I could learn to ride!

How much is a sidewalk worth? Much, much, more than you know or realize! Try it!!!!!

JOB, MY DOG

Once I had a dog named Job, a German Shepherd, a small one.
I understood there were papers for him. I never did get them.
Job had all the value he could have just being my friend!

Although he was small for a Shepherd, he was big for a lap dog;
and when he did jump up, you knew he was there. After he
settled down and looked up into your eyes, who cared! He would
lie there in his own gentle warm way just letting you know, "I'm
really your friend; I really want to be here." Except for needing
to go outside, he would stay there as long as he could and did!

I always felt Job was "my dog," and in a sense he was, but he
loved the rest of the family, too, the two children and Mom, I could
tell.

Job did get along with most everyone. Out at the lake
cabin he would play and be played with by the children
up and down the shore. He was a good pet, loyal friend;
and everyone seemed to like him.

When he came to where you were sitting; or when he
jumped on your lap, he would nuzzle you with his nose
wanting to be petted. He really didn't have to do that. He
could not be resisted anyhow.

There was in our household another "K-9," a small
white poodle named Gidget. She had been with the
family several years and had grown up with our girls, not
larger, just more mature. She was really part of the
family from her first Christmas when she was so small
she looked like a mouse. Gidget and Job did get along; each knew their
place, each had us all trained, and we loved them!

Job's big brown eyes were set in a marvelously colored head, his
mostly lustrous black coat splashed just right in light tan and some
white markings that were put there, I'm sure, by God's best designer.
Regardless of how he looked, his gentle yet positive personality, along
with those big brown eyes, made him "master of the house."

Job shared our lives for many wonderful years until one time that
we had to leave him tied outside in his "under the porch" house. Job
liked to ride, just bounding for the car when we went. He really felt he
was part of the family, and he loved to go for rides!

It had been a long day. Returning that evening, we found that Job had
chewed on the wood steps getting splinters in his throat. The rest of the
family had to take him to the vet. I could not!

Job left our family, but he left us with many fond memories! I miss
him to this day!

HUMOROUS WISDOM

" JEST A MINUTE"

Jest for a minute, an hour or a day. Some people live their whole lives that way!

"Be serious," we say, "get real," as if being serious and real have more appeal.

I think" jest a minute" is not too bad, certainly a lot better than feeling sad!!

Let's all jest a minute and make it last, and make unhappiness a thing of the past!!! Ha! Ha! Ha!

****

JUST YOU AND ME

Was I ready, really ready? It was time to go, time to decide, time to act. Was I ready???

I could not change the time or the circumstance. I could not run away; I could not even hide or deny; I had no choice, no where to go, no one else to pass to or blame. It was just you and me, Lord!

GUIDE TO TRAVELERS

1. Breathe!
2. Get up out of bed.
3. Go to the bathroom.
4. Thank God for the afore.
5. Start to think?
6. Get dressed.
7. Make big decisions about breakfast:
8. Make breakfast a conference meal:
   Where shall we go today?
   How are we going to get there?
   When shall we start?
9. Stop arguing!
10. Go to the bathroom.
11. Just Go.
12. Enjoy.
13. When to stop for lunch?
14. Where to stop for lunch?
15. Stop arguing!
16. Just stop.
17. Eat.
18. Go to the bathroom.
19. Hit the road.
20. Repeat for evening meal:
    Where?
    When?
    Go to the bathroom.
21. Hit the road.
22. When to stop for the night?
23. Where to stop for the night?
24. Stop arguing!!
25. Just stop.
26. What to do before bed?
    Snacks?
    T.V.- what program?
    What time to go to bed?
    What time to get up?
27. Stop arguing!!!!!!!
28. Go to the bathroom.
29. Go to bed.
30. Thank God for the day, and
    pray for a good night's rest.
31. Start over with #1. (Good luck!)

ORDER

There needs to be an order for things, like happiness, for instance. "One order of happiness, please. Make that extra large!"

People in general are not the best at following orders. Now-a-days, rather they, do they question, question without even necessarily wanting to know the answer. They question because if they do, they can get away with not doing anything!

They say the "order" is not good enough; it should be better, even though they offer no specific suggestions. It is enough so that they, again, do not have to do anything!

They cannot physically or mentally do it, and "trying" just is not in their vocabulary. They will never find out, but they know there are a lot of other people who can.

There are many excuses people use as reasons for not following an order. There just is not enough paper to put them on!

The fact is, the only good order is the one that is followed, no matter what; for following is trying, and one should always try.

To think, to try to do the best you can, should be the order of your day!

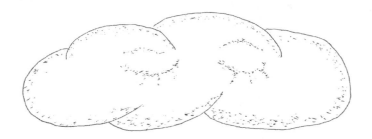

REAL VALUE

Does it need to be something you can touch to be something you love so much?

Do you have to feel that it is real before it has your attention and appeal?

Must an object be seen to make it keen and have value in your eyes?

Well, then take a cloud – for crying out loud- as it floats so lazy in the skies,

Holding whatever shape or form you imagine in your mind,

A creation knowing no limits, that is such a wonderful find

For all to share, all who care, to appreciate the beauty created.

For God's will is with us still, His mercy and grace for us first-rated!

WATER BUG

Water bug, water bug , skiddering around right on top of the water he could be found!
Darting here, darting there, darting all around without a single care!
"How can you do that?" one would ask. "Cause I'm a water bug, for me it's no task!"
Well ,on the water he may be able to walk, but I'm the one able to talk!
All God's creatures have their place. There is much more than just the human race!
We all have our talents and things we can do that the good Lord wants us to share,
For we were created to live together; that means we all have to care!
So skidder, you water bug, while you may; you could well help a fish one day! Gulp!

****

GNAT

If I were a gnat so tiny and small, I would almost feel like nothing at all! Who really sees me? Who really does care? I'm just so small most are unaware, but give me a break; God knows me, too! He has given me a home just like you! I may be small, but after all, I still can hear and answer God's call!
All God's creatures, regardless of size, were created by God, the one most wise, to share this earth, to use its wealth, to use it all for our good health, side by side with respect for all, living and sharing till God's last call!

"SPACE PEACE"

There is a certain peace when you
are away and viewing things at a distance,
as if that distance is between you and the
problems of life.

Perhaps that's why we all want our
"space", our very own space so we can
capture our problems, put them away,
and then leave.

Space for a problem does not get rid
of the problem; it just makes room for
more problems that need more space for
more problems!

It would be better to space them out
in the beginning, give them no space to
grow, saving all the room for positive things.
That would be better don't you know.

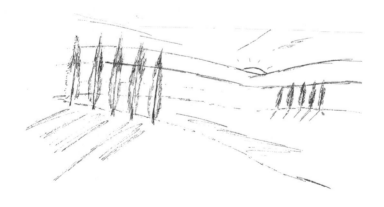

FUTURE

What exactly is future or the future? It is common to believe that it is what will happen from this day forward, and that's true!

Some may say the future is a given; some will say others control our future, even that God controls our future. While there may be some truth in some of "that stuff," the fact is we really do not know for sure. Even God, in His wisdom, has changed His mind, and so when we look to our future, we must realize that our future REACTS TO US, to our goals, to our choices, to our thoughts, and to our actions. We owe it to ourselves, therefore, to make the most of our God-given opportunities and thank God for our future!!

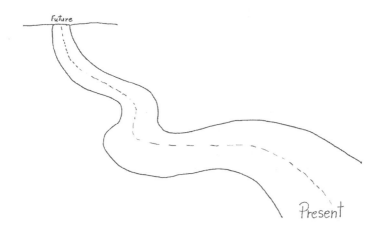

BEAR AND BUNNY

"I'M HUNGRY!" growled the big brown bear as he looked hungrily at the small plump hare!
"Well I don't care if you are!" said he. "I am not going to let you eat me."
Off he hopped, with big bear after, having such fun you could hear his laughter!!
Old big brown got tired at last; the bunny always knew that he was too fast!
To tell the truth the bunny said to me, "we really are good friends don't you see!! Hop, Ha, Hop, Ha!"

~~~~~~~~~~~~~~~~~~~~~~~~~~~~~~~~~~~~

TWEETER BIRD AND BUMBLE BEE

Tweeter bird and bumble bee buzzed and flew around a tree,
each enjoying the fresh spring day, all in " their" own special way.
Tweeter looked for stuff to build his nest while bumble looked for the sweetest and the best!
They fluttered and buzzed all through the day; it was after all a warm day in May!
Spring is special for the birds and bees; it helps to make more you's and me's! (Hah)

GUN SHY

There was a little pistol; he was a son of a gun! He went off a lot, and did he have fun! His uncle was a big shot of the highest caliber. In winter he wore a coat of the finest fur. "Draw," said the pistol. "Beat me if you can." Most of them thought. Then away they ran! The little pistol now became a repeater; he just thought he wanted to be neater. The little repeater has retired now. To "no one" in his life did he ever bow!

KNOWLEDGE

Knowledge comes from learning; learning comes from studying; studying happens when we decide to do it. Knowledge comes from us and what we do to learn it. All the stories, the books, lectures, computers, or "whatever" mean nothing unless we listen, unless we accept with an open mind and process and evaluate. Then the biggest benefit of all is to use that knowledge to help others!

#'s

The number you press when you are in distress is 911, don't you know!

The result you get if you keep your wit is an emergency place to go, where they care for your ills, maybe give you pills to help you endure your pain!

It's all for the best, the best in the west, with only your health to gain!

"DOODLE"?

She likes to doodle; it comes from her noodle; on paper she puts it all!

I like to see what she does for me, illustrating how to have a ball!

Imagination that's found in her is profound and the results a reward of their own!

Let your mind drift as she gives you a lift, and her generosity is generously shown!

CARING

Caring is a personal thing. It is sometimes said when someone does something, "Who cares?" Well, if you as a person do not care, "Who will?" Caring comes from someone and shows concern, and concern is needed so that we will care. Caring has the power to change. Caring can make all the difference in the world. We must use care with caring, but we must always care!

****

HANDS

Hands have many uses. There are many sayings that use hands such as "Hands up!" "It's in your hands.", "To the hands that rock the cradle!" etc. Every saying, every thought has to do with the hands doing something.

We should look at our own hands and see what they are doing and remember the saying about "idle hands."

The most powerful hands are the hands folded in prayer!

LAUGHTER

Laughter makes the heart sing, and to the eye brings a tear;
Gives music to the soul and happiness to all those here.
To laugh with your heart and let your soul sing,
Gives peace to your life; it's the best of everything!

LIFE'S PURPOSE

What better purpose is there to life, than life with a purpose?
What better purpose for my life than living with a purpose?
What better purpose than to live my life for my purpose?
What better purpose for my life than to live my life fully?
How better to live my life fully than to share my life fully?
I purposely intend to do just that!

"Life is all there is to life."

QUIET TIME

Quiet time comes when your world is at peace. It does not always need the absence of noise! Quiet time comes when your mind is still and your heart is at rest. Quiet times come to your soul when you feel the presence of God in your life!

THRILLS

Thrills happen when the body and mind are challenged and through your action or thought you do something out of the ordinary, different, or perhaps somewhat daring. You think it, you do it, and the accomplishment gives you the shivers! It's a thrill!

TOGETHERNESS

Togetherness, to be sure, is not being alone, and I will tell you now that God is always with us!
In this earthly life there is a need for us to be together with another human being, someone who has the same feelings, goals, faults, strengths and weaknesses, someone vulnerable and imperfect like us. We need to be together to understand how we feel, each giving comfort and strength to the other!

KEEP PLAYING!

There are big children and big kids, and when they play its hard to say which has the most fun!
The lines of age melt together; joy and laughter prevail!
Life is the continued practice of youth, and age is relevant.
Fear not, moms, dads, grandparents, all big kids keep playing; try to get it right!
May you never get it right.
May your play be out of sight!
May the happiness it will bring,
Make you dear old heart sing!!! Puff! Puff!

****

FAMILY AND FRIENDS

Food, laughter, family, and friends,
make for memories that know no ends.
Joy being shared by people who care;
I thank the Lord that I was there!

SETTING THE TIME

We buy a new watch, and we set the time, for one reason or another. Some may set it faster, perhaps even slower in our attempt to use time to our advantage!

God is really the one who sets our time, and His time is always the right time!

In sporting events when time runs out, the game is over! In our life here on earth, when our earthly time runs out, God promises us, through faith, eternal life!

We never really lose those we love in the faith because that faith will bring us together again for all eternity!

The celebration of a game victory lasts only a short time. The celebration of God's victory over death lasts for life eternal!!

The question why, God answers, in his correct time, with the gift of eternal life?

Lord, help us celebrate your victory over death! Amen